HTML

For Beginners

A Complete Beginners HTML Guide to Developing a
Strong Coding Foundation and Mastering the Fundamentals
of Modern Web Design

By

Ethan Hall

trademarks and brands within this book are for clarifying purposes only and are owned by the owner, not affiliated with this document.

Table of Contacts

Introduction

You adore the Web, and if you've read this far, you do as well. Around the same time, the Internet is complex, noisy, thrilling, interesting, and useful. From a user's perspective, the Internet is a lot of fun, but that's just half of the picture. The Internet's participatory nature is maybe its strongest feature. You can create your material — a tree! It's incredible. There has never been a contact system like this. Anyone with a basic PC and a little experience will start their home-stead over one of the most thrilling networks in the development of communication.

The main issue is figuring out what to do. Often website development books are just about learning how to use apps that you have to purchase. That's well, but it's not needed. Many software programs have emerged to render web creation simpler — and some of them perform very well — but regardless of the software product you use, you also need to understand what's going on beneath the surface. It is where this book enters the image.

This book would teach you everything you need to know about the Internet. You'll learn how to use various apps, but most importantly, you'll build your web page.

You'll find out:

You'll learn how websites are made and the fundamental layout of web pages. Since you create your pages, you'll have a good understanding of the structure. There are no enigmas online.

What is the difference between substance and style? You'll grasp the fundamental tenet of contemporary Internet thinking: that style and substance can be kept apart.

How to use network standards: The Internet is a jumbled mess, but out of the chaos, several standards have emerged. You'll learn how these standards function and how to put them to use.

How to make attractive web pages: By default, you want the website to look great. You'll learn how to use shape, pattern, color, and photographs in this book.

How to create modern layouts: Several websites have tables, lists, and other fancy elements. You'll work out where to build it.

Add Interactive elements: The other languages enable you to add forms to your websites, validate form details, and create animations.

Chapter-1 Overview of HTML

Tim Berners-Lee, a scientist at the CERN science institute in Switzerland, coined HTML. He introduced the concept of a hypertext structure built on the Internet. HTML is abbreviated as Hypertext Markup Language. It helps the user build and structure lines, chapters, headings, connections, and blockquotes for websites and applications.

HTML isn't a programming language, so it can't do anything like build complex functionality. Instead, it allows you to arrange and type papers in the same way as Microsoft Word does.

The most commonly used language for writing Web pages is HTML. The way Websites (HTML documents) are connected referred to as Hypertext. As a result, the relation accessible on a website is referred to as Hypertext.

HTML stands for Hypertext Markup Language, which means you can use it to "markup" textual content with tags that inform a Web viewer how to view it. HTML was created to describe the layout of documents such as headings, paragraphs, indexes, and so on to make scientific knowledge more easily shared amongst researchers. HTML is also commonly used to structure web pages using the various tags included in the HTML language, such as <article>, <header>, and <footer>.

1.1 How Does HTML Work?

HTML archives are files with the extensions.html and.htm. Any web browser can be used to use them (such as Safari, Mozilla Firefox or Google Chrome). The HTML file is interpreted by the browser, which renders the material for internet users to see. Typically, a website would have many separate HTML sections. About pages, email pages and Home pages for example, will have their own HTML records. Each HTML page is made up of a series of tags (also known as elements), which can be thought of as the web page's building blocks. They organize the material into pages, headings, chapters, and other content blocks using a hierarchy. The <tag> </tag> syntax is used for the opening and closing of most HTML objects. Here's an illustration of how HTML components should be organized in code:

```
<div>
<h2>The Heading</h2>
<h3>Sun heading</h3>
<p>One Paragraph</p>
<img src="/" alt="picture">
<p>It is paragraph-2 <a href="https://google.com">hyper_link</a></p>
</div>
```

The final aspect is a basic division (div>/div>) that can be used to separate larger material pieces. A heading (h1>/h1>), a subheading (h2>/h2>), two paragraphs (p>/p>), and a graphic (img>) are all included. A connect (a>/a>) with a href element that contains the target URL is used in the second paragraph. There are two other attributes on the image tag: src for the picture direction and alt and picture definition.

1.2 Most Used HTML Tags

H inline tags and Block-level are the two kinds of HTML tags. Block-level components take up the entire usable room in the document and often launch a new line. Block tags are often seen in headings and paragraphs. Inline components just take as much room as they require and do not break the page's flow. They're used to format the inside contents of block-level objects. Inline tags include things like links and highlighted strings. HTML's Advantages and Disadvantages HTML, like other products, has its own set of advantages and disadvantages.

Advantages:

A commonly spoken language with a large population and a wealth of capital. Every web browser supports it natively. It has a simple learning curve. It's fully free and open-source.

Markup that is neat and reliable. The w3c is in charge of maintaining official web specifications Back - end technologies such as Node. Js and PHP are easily integrated.

Build a website - If you learn HTML well, you can build a website or customize an established design. Become a web developer - HTML and CSS programming is a must-have experience if you choose to pursue a career as a talented web designer.

Understand the Internet - If you'd like to improve the pace and functionality of your website, you should be familiar with HTML. Learn another language - After you've mastered the fundamentals of HTML, you'll find many other similar technologies such as JavaScript, PHP, and Angular become even simpler to grasp.

Disadvantages:

Static websites are the majority of the time. You can use PHP and JAVA for dynamic features. It prevents the consumer from implementing logic. Consequently, even though they use the same components, such as headers and footers, each web page must be generated separately. Any browsers are reluctant to implement new features.

Browser behavior may be unpredictable (for example, older browsers don't often make newer tags).

1.3 HTML's Applications

HTML is among the most commonly known programming languages on the Internet. You will study a couple of them below:

- Web page creation - HTML is a markup language that is used to generate websites. About any web page contains HTML tags, which render the page's information in a window.

- Internet Routing - HTML offers tags for navigating from one link to the next, and it is widely used for internet routing.

- Flexible UI - HTML sites already run on all platforms, including phones, tablets, desktops, and notebooks, thanks to responsive design.

- Offline access HTML pages will be made accessible remotely, mostly on the machine, without the requirement for an internet connection after they have been loaded.

- Game creation- HTML5 has built-in support for rich experiences and is now useful in game development.

1.4 HTML's Various Versions

HTML 1.0

HTML 1.0 was the first edition of HTML. It had many limitations in terms of functionality, which restricted what you're doing with your websites.

HTML 2.0

Then came HTML 2.0, which contained many HTML 1.0 and a few different ones for web design. HTML 2.0 has been the industry norm for web page design until January 1997.

HTML 3.0

HTML 2.0 performed its mission admirably, but many web page designers (also known as HTML writers or webmasters) desired greater influence of their pages and more opportunities to label up the text and improve the appearance with the sites. Netscape, the most popular browser, launched the Netscape Extension Tags, collecting new tags and attributes. Other browsers attempted to copy them, but since Netscape could not thoroughly define their new tags, they did not fit with any other browsers. When HTML developers were using these attributes and tags and then discovered that they didn't fit as intended in other browsers, it caused many frustration and issues. Around the same period, an HTML task force headed by Dave Raggett released the HTML 3.0 draught, which featured a slew of fresh and helpful features. However, only a few items from this draught were introduced in most browsers. The term "HTML 3.0 improved" soon gained popularity on the Internet but is mostly applied to documents with browser-specific tags rather than documents that followed the HTML 3.0 draft. One of the factors the draught was shelved was because of this. HTML 3.0 isn't any longer in use. Another factor HTML 3.0 didn't cut was that it was too "tall." Future versions were to be implemented in a much more "modular" manner, allowing browsers to adopt them bit by bit or modular by modular.

HTML 3.2

HTML 3.2 is the latest version of HTML (WILBUR). With the introduction of more browser-specific tags, it became clear that a new standard was needed. The W3C, which was formed in 1994 to create universal specifications for Web development, introduced the WILBUR specification, which came to be known as HTML 3.2, as a result. HTML 3.2 reflects the prescribed norm as of early 1996, and it was adopted as an accepted system in January 1997. HTML 3.2 is supported by the majority, if not all, of today's mainstream browsers.

HTML 4.0

HTML 4.0 was script COUGAR in its early days. This update adds additional features, the majority of which are derived from the now-defunct HTML 3.0 draught. In December 1997, this edition was designated as a guideline, and in April 1998, it was designated as a norm. Explorer has done an excellent job in integrating HTML 4.0's several functions. Regrettably, Netscape hasn't kept up. The new edition of Netscape Communicator also doesn't accept many of the HTML 4.0 tags and attributes. It ensures that a new website with HTML 4.0 basic tags will look fantastic in Explorer but will look terrible in Netscape.

XHTML (Extensible Hypertext Markup Language)

You'd imagine that after HTML 4.0, the next big version will be HTML 5.0, which will have a slew of different tags capable of doing all kinds of amazing stuff. It would be an excellent estimate, but it would be incorrect. After HTML 4, XHTML is the next edition of HTML. Extensible Hypertext Mark-up Language XHTML is an acronym for Configurable Hypertext Markup Language. XHTML isn't taking several different tags with it. XHTML aims to counter the latest browser innovations that are sweeping the globe. Web sites are also viewed in browsers on cell phones, automobiles, televisions, and various other hand-held digital computers and communicators. Alternative internet connectivity methods are constantly being implemented. These machines, in many situations, lack the processing capacity of a laptop or desktop machine and therefore are unable to handle weak or careless coding activities. XHTML addresses these developments. XHTML frequently addresses the requirement for disabled people (such as the blind) to provide internet connectivity. As a result, web pages published in XHTML can be used on various web and internet sites.

XHTML is the culmination of the World Wide Web Consortium's (W3C) tireless efforts to provide a format for delivering rich, high-quality web pages through a wide range of devices. In January of 2000, the World Wide Web Consortium (W3C) made XHTML an approved suggestion. XHTML is the latest version of HTML that is becoming an online standard.

HTML 5

The next version of HTML.HTML 5 (commonly abbreviated as HTML5) is the latest online format. It is based on HTML 4 (which was released in 1997) or XHTML. A lot happened on the site since the launch of HTML4, and more remains to be improved to fix all of the emerging technology and multimedia. HTML5 is the product of a collaboration between the W3C and the Internet WHATWG that started in 2006. Although HTML5 is still in progress, all of the current functionality and features are supported by the most recent browsers. HTML5's main goal is to do two things: develop the vocabulary and promote the most up-to-date multimedia. The WHATWG and W3C developed certain ground standards to do this. Reduced reliance on external sockets improved error management, and much more markup tags to substitute scripting were among them. HTML5 should be platform agnostic (that is, it should be interpreted by machines and the various applications that occur today) while still being understandable by humans.

1.5 HTML Editor

In retrospect, the HTML editor is being used to build a website's base. And just because any text editor may do the job doesn't mean you want to do it yourself. Added features, error-correcting, and an overall more intuitive editor will greatly simplify your life. HTML editors have the same fundamentals: they assist you in writing code by illustrating grammar, inserting frequently encountered HTML components and constructs, and delivering autocompletion.

Text may be converted to other languages utilizing an HTML editor, such as XML, JavaScript or CSS. However, as You all know, not everything is created equal. Some editors may be simpler to use than others, and some may have more features.

1.6 Types HTML Editor

To put it another way, still! For both novice and experienced developers, an HTML editor is essential. The main components of HTML editors, such as syntax highlighting, adding popular HTML components, and autocompletion, have already been listed. All of this ensures that the code remains usable and tidy with minimal effort, making it far simpler to be doing what you should do the best code.

If you fail to put the ending tag / in a code feature, e.g., the editor will warn you. As a result, you need not restrict yourself by not having an HTML editor.

1.7 Atom

Atom is an HTML editor released in 2014 and has gained a lot of popularity since then. The GitHub team created Atom, which is a free, accessible code editor. Atom's kit is released under a free software license and is operated by the GitHub group. It aims to give the editor a premium feel while remaining fully accessible. Often included is the ability to configure the app. In terms of the tagline, they tout themselves as an easy to hack text document for the twenty-first century. It ensures that developers can further boost Atom by editing, extending, changing, sharing the program's source code, and creating their packages.

Let's go over some of Atom's main features.

Characteristics

- Atom comes including 81 pre-installed packages and allows you to load up to 8,700 more. You may even create your software.

- A text editor that is free and open-source. The Atom editor is completely free and open-source, and it can be found on GitHub.

- Atom assists teletype. If you want to collaborate with other programmers in real-time, this is a crucial function.

- Multiple panes are supported. Atom will divide the interface into several windows, allowing you to analyze and write code in parallel.

- Intelligent autocompletion. Atoms versatile autocomplete makes you write code quicker and smarter.

- Atom is common with web developers because it is customizable. Atom is simple to customize, allowing you to change the appearance of the GUI and incorporate other useful features. You may also build your own sets and themes. Alternatively, you should easily install community-made packages and themes.

- Atom in Developer Mode You can play around with the main framework by introducing new functionality.

- Integration of Git and GitHub.

- Editing on many platforms. Atom is compatible with all operating systems.

- Atom has a sleek, premium-looking interface, as well as a live demo. Windows, Linux and Mac OS are all supported (64-bit).

1.8 Notepad ++

Notepad++ is indeed a free HTML editor designed for Windows-based computers. Wine allows Linux users to access it as well. This editor is licensed as free software, and its source code can be found on GitHub. Third-party extensions are funded, much as with other group initiatives. The versatility of Notepad++'s programming framework sets it apart. Notepad++ is very lightweight, with a smartphone edition available if you choose. Here are a few of the highlights:

Characteristics

- Notepad++ has a user interface that is plain, lightweight, and fast.

- It has a multilingual coding environment that includes ActionScript, CSS, and Visual Simple.

- Complete compliance for Windows; however, most operating systems are not allowed (without additional software.)

Why do developers like Notepad++ so much?

- It's open-source and free; • It's extensible. You may use community-created plugins or make your own.

- It's adaptable. Developers can customize the functionality and design to their liking.

- The Notepad++ GUI is easy, but developers can customize it. Windows and Linux are supported (via Wine)

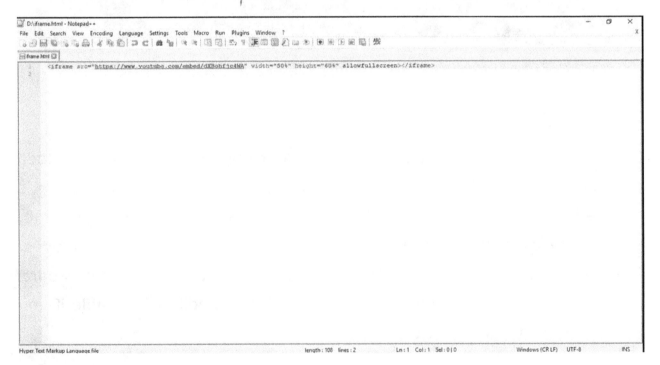

1.9 Sublime Text

Another great free HTML editor is Sublime Text. This app, which was created by either a Sydney-based company, falls into the freemium range.

Sublime text is freemium, which ensures you can download it for free but must purchase a license to use any of its functionality.

Sublime provides excellent assistance to guarantee that the package is still up to date. Users may use community-made plugins or create their own. You believe that the free edition of Sublime is sufficient. However, if you find that you want additional functionality, you can purchase the license later.

Characteristics

- Python API is supported by Sublime, allowing the plugin to extend its default features.

- Editing in real-time. You may make modifications to a large number of locations at once.

- It is cross-platform. Sublime is a text editor that runs on Windows, Linux or Mac OS X. Sublime Text 2 developers only require one license to use it on any of their machines. Sublime text is common with web developers for several reasons.

- A robust API ecosystem and package ecosystem. Thousands of bundles are accessible and designed by the group for Sublime. These programs are free and open-source.

- Editing in two sections. Developers may use several displays to work on various forms of programming at the same time.

- Go everywhere. This function is useful for quickly opening files and searching for icons, lines, or terms.

- Sublime automatically indexes the definition of Go to Any class, process, and feature in your project.

- In terms of aesthetics, the Sublime Text GUI is fantastic. Windows, Linux or Mac (32/64 bit) are both supported.

1.10 Adobe Dreamweaver CC

Dreamweaver would be a premium, strong, and scalable tool developed and operated by software giant Adobe Inc. It offers both back-end and front-end production services. Dreamweaver is a closed-source application that is built to run inside the Adobe ecosystem. Adobe also offers tools, features, and plugins to ensure that you can write consistently. One of the editors who supports both WYSIWYG and textual approaches is Dreamweaver. So, you have the option of coding for a live video demonstration or going the traditional route.

Characteristics

- You can write code in every big programming language with Dreamweaver.

- WYSIWYG and Textual editor modes are supported.

- The Adobe app environment is fully integrated.

- Adobe Inc. provided excellent performance and assistance.

Why do web designers and developers like Adobe Dreamweaver CC?

- Create a code and test it. Developers will code when displaying the final product in this manner.

- Double-check the coding and the page's usability. This functionality will help developers adhere to the Web-Content Accessibility Guidelines more easily (WCAG.)

- Access to cloud-based creative libraries. Premium subscription to the Adobe ecosystem's vast library of assets. Colors, sentences, animations, layers, characters, and more are all included.

- Dreamweaver has a premium, high-end style about it, with a breathtaking aesthetic and architecture. After all, it's from Adobe, a well-known name inside the creative industry.

- Windows and Mac OS X are supported.

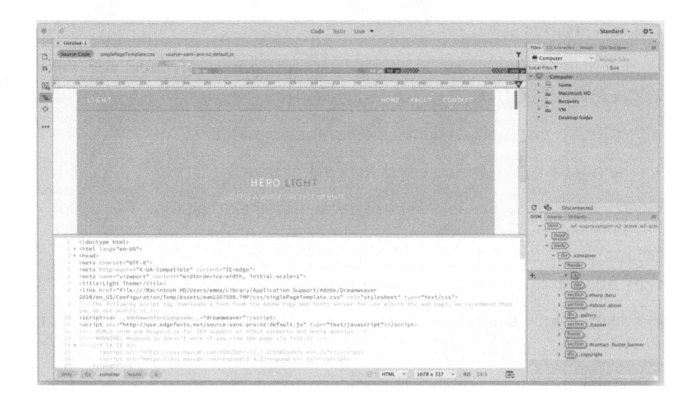

1.11 Visual Studio Code

With a vast number of customizable features, it is a free multi-code HTML editor ready to use. It takes pride in its intelligent autocomplete and other syntax answers. Visual Studio is a multi-platform and multi-language application. Its creation framework is compatible with HTML, Python, and a variety of other programming languages. It's also compliant with Microsoft Azure, allowing for simple deployment and a wide range of extensions.

Characteristics

- IntelliSense encourages you to move beyond autocomplete and syntax highlighting. It generates intelligent completions for you based on your forms, tasks, and modules.

- Features and customization. Install plugins and connect languages, styles, debuggers, and other features to your device.

- You can quickly move between different tasks thanks to the project manager's easy accessibility.

- Visual Studio Code is a favorite of web developers for several reasons.

- You can debug the code directly in the editor.

- Git commands are pre-installed. Work with Git suppliers from the editor when editing diffs, staging archives, and other files.

- The Live Server extension allows you to see a live version of your web app when editing it.

- Visual Studio has a traditional style with a clean and straightforward layout. It allows finding documents, installing a new language, and opening a new file easy. Windows x64, Linux x64 and OSX x64 are also supported.

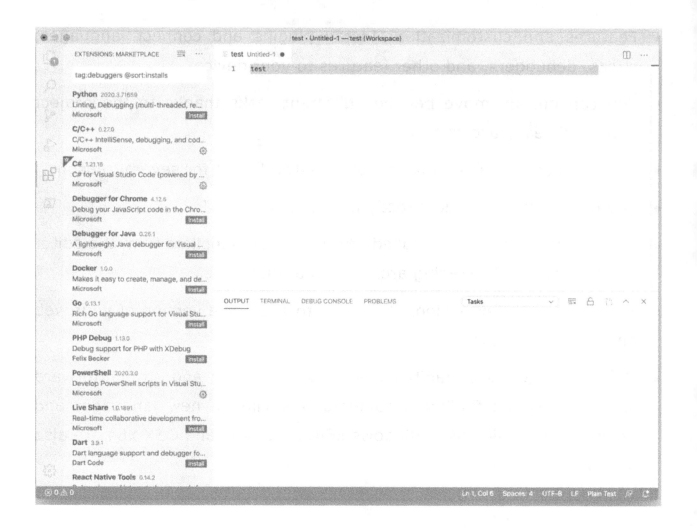

1.12 HTML statistics and figures

- Since the mid-1990s, the HTML, head, and body components were components of the HTML specification, and they were the key elements used to format HTML documents until a few years ago. Thanks to HTML5's addition of a slew of modern tags that can attach rich textual context to an HTML document's layout, the situation has improved significantly in recent years.

- HTML documents must begin with such a Document-Type Declaration (also known as a "doctype"). The doctype is used in browsers to describe the rendering mode. Since HTML5 does not describe a DTD, the doctype declaration in HTML5 is clearer and shorter.

- Since mobile browsers have completely implemented HTML5, building mobile-ready designs are as simple as designing and building for their small touch screen screens, which is why Responsive Design is so common. Some excellent meta tags enable you to customize for mobile devices as well.

- Seventy-eight percent of content creators believe the framework is appropriate for developing smartphone applications, and 68 percent believe it is appropriate for building any of all types of apps.

- HTML5 also has a slew of useful APIs for creating a smoother user interface and a more robust, dynamic web framework — here's a fast rundown of native APIs:

- Offline storage folder • Browser history tracking • Document editing • Timed video replay

- A single entity doesn't regulate HTML5. The reality is an accessible norm is one of its strongest qualities. Developers are free to let their imaginations run wild and incorporate as many features and functions as they want.

- Unlike some apps, Google Chrome ensures that any upgrade includes HTML5 support. Furthermore, YouTube's default player is already HTML5, and Google's Flash advertisements are upgraded to HTML5.

Developers' use of HTML5 (by region):

- North America uses 70 percent

- South America uses 61 percent

- ASPAC uses 60 percent

- Australia uses 60 percent

- Europe uses 59 percent

- Africa uses 50 percent

Chapter-2 Elements & Attributes in HTML

Consequent rise or properties of an entity, such as the widths and height of an image, are defined by attributes. Attributes are often defined in the opening tag and are usually name/value pairs such as name="value." Quote markers can still be used around attribute values.

Some attributes are often expected for some components. An <img> tag, for example, must have alt and src attributes. Let's glance at several explanations of how attributes should be used:

```
<image src="Scope.png" width="80" height="80" alt="School">
```

```
<a href="https://www.instagram.com/" title="HTML">
```

```
Instagram </a>
```

```
<abbr title="United States of America">USA </abbr>
```

```
input type="Integer" value="54126">
```

In the illustration above, src is an attribute within the <img> tag, and the picture path is its value. Similarly, the attribute href or within <a> tag is also an attribute, and the meaning is the relation given, and so on.

Attribute attributes may be quoted with single or double-quotes. Double quotations, on the other hand, are the most frequent. When the attribute value includes double quotes, the value must be wrapped in single quotes, for example, value='John "Williams" Jr.' In the illustration above, src is an attribute within the <img> tag, and picture path is its value. Similarly, the attribute href within the <a> tag is an attribute, and the meaning is the relation given, and so on. Attribute attributes may be quoted with single or double-quotes. Double quotations, on the other hand, are the most frequent.

When the attribute value includes double quotes, the value must be wrapped in single quotes, for example, value='John "Williams" Jr.'

A few HTML attributes don't have name/value pairs and have the name. Boolean attributes are the name for certain types of attributes. Verified, disabled, read-only, necessary, and other similar Boolean attributes are examples.

As an example

```
<input type="E-mail" required>
```

```
<Input Type= " Add" value "add" disable>
```

```
<input type="Charter" value="Read Character" read_only>
```

Many of these elements would be covered in depth in the following pages. Except for the Class and id attributes, which are case-sensitive, attribute values are usually case-insensitive. In their definition, the W3C (World Wide Web Consortium) proposes using lowercase for attribute values.

2.1 Attributes for a General Purpose

You may use certain attributes on the maximum of HTML objects, such as class, id, title and type. The following segment explains how to use them.

2.2 The "id" Attribute

An id attribute is being used to assign an entity in a document a special meaning or identifier. This allows CSS or JavaScript selection of the element much simpler.

```
<input type="Enter Text " id="First_Name">
```

```
<div id="Roll. No">
```

```
Some details </div>
```

```
<p id="information's Text">
```

```
First Paragraph. </p>
```

Within a single text, an element's id must be special. There can't be two elements of the same id in the same text because each entity can only have one id.

2.3 The class Attribute

The class attribute, like the id attribute, is used to define elements. The class attribute, unlike the id attribute, does not need to be special within the code. As seen in the following illustration, you may add a same class for multiple items in a text.

```
<input type="Enter text" class=" city">
```

```
<div class="City">New York</div>
```

```
<p class="city ">NY is beautiful city. </p>
```

Since a class may be extended to several elements, any style guidelines written for it will be assigned to any of the elements with that class.

2.4 The "style" Attribute

The style attribute enables you to define CSS styling rules directly inside the feature, such as color, font, border, and so on. To see where it operates, consider the following example:

```
<p style="color: Green;">First Paragraph. </p>
```

```
<img src="image/facebook.png " style="width: 500px;" alt="Logo">
```

```
<div style="border: 2px black ;">Facebook </div>
```

2.5 Accept Attribute

The allow attribute determines which file types the server can accept (which can be added through upload of file).

Only input <type="file"> may be used with the accept attribute. This attribute cannot be used as a validation function. On the website, file uploads must be validated.

```
<form action="/action_page.html">
```

```
<input type="file" name="picture" accepts="Photo/*">
```

```
<input type="submitted">
```

```
</form>
```

2.6 Accept-charset Attribute

The accept-charset attribute defines the word encodings that would be used when submitting the form. The reserved variable "UNKNOWN" (which means that the encoding matches the encoding of the file outlining the <form> element) is the default value.

```
<form action="/action_page.html" accept-charset=" utf-8">
```

```
First_Name: <input type="Enter text" name="F_name"><br>
```

```
Last_Name: <input type="Enter text" name="L-name"><br>
```

```
<input type="Add" value="Add">
```

```
</form>
```

2.7 "Accesskey" Attribute

The "<accesskey" attribute identifies a shortcut key used to unlock or concentrate an element. In different browsers, the shortcuts key is accessed in multiple ways.

Browser	Windows	Linux	Mac
Internet Explorer	[Alt] + *accesskey*	N/A	
Chrome	[Alt] + *accesskey*	[Alt] + *accesskey*	[Control] [Alt] + *accesskey*
Firefox	[Alt] [Shift] + *accesskey*	[Alt] [Shift] + *accesskey*	[Control] [Alt] + *accesskey*
Safari	[Alt] + *accesskey*	N/A	[Control] [Alt] + *accesskey*
Opera	Opera 15 or newer: [Alt] + *accesskey* Opera 12.1 or older: [Shift] [Esc] + *accesskey*		

2.8 The "title" Attribute

The title attribute indicates the element's title. The title attribute's syntax is identical to that of the id attribute:

This attribute's behavior is determined by the element that contains it, but it is often shown as a tooltip while the cursor passes over the component or when it is loading.

E.g.

```
<html>
```

```
<head>  < title>The tit</title> </head>
```

```
<body>
```

```
<h3 title="HTML!">It is the title</h3>
```

```
</body>
```

```
</html>
```

As a consequence, you'll get the following: It is the title.

When you hover your mouse on " It is the title, " you'll see that the title you used during your code appears as a tooltip for the cursor.

2.9 The "dir" Attribute

The "dir" attribute helps you to tell the browser which way the text can flow. As seen in the table below, the "dir" attribute will follow one of two values:

- ltr (left- right) (the default value)

- rtl Right- left (languages such as Arabic or Hebrew which are read or write right hand side to left hand side)

Example

```
<html dir="rtl">
```

```
<head>
```

```
<title>Title here</title>
```

```
</head>
```

```
<body>
```

```
The is an example from right to left
```

```
</body>
```

```
</html>
```

As a consequence, you'll get the following. It is an example from right to left. When the "dir" attribute is included in the html> tag, it controls how text is shown in the document. When included inside another tag, it directs the text for the material of that tag only.

2.10 The lang Attribute

The lang attribute lets you choose the primary language in a text, but it's just in HTML for expandable storage with older language versions. In modern XHTML papers, this attribute has been substituted by the XML: lang attribute. The lang attribute accepts ISO 639-1.two-character language codes as values. For a full set of language codes, see Codes: ISO 639-1

Example

```
<html lang="Code">
<head>
<title>HTML Page </title>
</head>
<body> This is first page of HTML </body>
</html>
```

The XML: lang Attribute is used to specify the language of a document. The XML: lang attribute takes the role of the lang attribute in XHTML. As discussed in the previous part, the type of an XML: lang attribute is an ISO-639-1 country code.

2.11 alt Attribute

Suppose a user is unable to open a picture for any purpose. In that case, the alt attribute offers alternate content (because of slow internet connection, an error in the src Parameter, or if you are using the screen reader). For the <img> variable, the alt parameter is needed. The alt attribute for <input> elements may only be used for input type="image"> elements. Use the title parameter to make a preview for a picture!

Example

```
<img src="Earth.gif" width="60" height="60" alt="Google-Map"
use-map="#Google-map">
<map name="Earth">
  <area shape="Squre" coords="10,10,182,226" href="school.htm" alt="mars">
  <area shape="rect" coords="80,158,13" href="habib0.htm" alt="Sun">
  <area shape="rect" coords="124,158,18" href="moon.htm" alt="Moon">
</map>
```

2.12 HTML elements

One of many types of HTML nodes, an HTML element is a form of Hypertext Markup Language) file part (there are comment nodes, text nodes, and others). An HTML document comprises a tree of basic HTML nodes, like HTML elements and text nodes that give the document semantics and formatting (e.g., make text bold, organize it into lists, paragraphs and embed hyperlinks or tables and images). HTML attributes may be defined for each feature. Content may also be added to elements, such as other components and text.

<HTML> (Hypertext Markup Language)

The core (top-level portion) of an Html page is described by the HTML <html> element, often known as the primary root. This aspect must be the ancestor of all other components.

<base>

The HTML <base> element specify the base URL for all relative Web addresses in a document.

<head>

Machine-readable details (metadata) about the text, such as its scripts, title and style sheets, is contained in the HTML <head> element.

<link>

The HTML External Reference Link (<link>) feature establishes a connection between the document window and an external resource. This feature is most widely used to connect to CSS, but it can also create site icons (all "favicon" type icons and symbols for the main screen and applications on mobile devices).

<meta>

Metadata which can be expressed by other HTML context items, such as foundation, relation, script, type, or title, is represented by the HTML <meta> feature.

<styling>

The HTML <style> variable specifies the style of a document or a section of a document.

<title>

The HTML Title variable (<title>) specifies the document title that appears in the title bar of a browser or the tab of a website.

2.13 Content sectioning

You may use information sectioning elements to divide the document's content into logical parts. Build a broad overview of your page's content using the sectioning elements, which provide footer and header navigation and heading elements to define content parts.

<address>

The HTML <address> aspect denotes that the embedded HTML contains contact details for individuals or groups of individuals or a business.

<article>

The HTML <article> feature denotes a self-contained structure in a book, page, program, or website intended to be distributed or reused separately (e.g., in syndication).

<aside>

The HTML <aside> aspect denotes a section of a document that material is only tangentially linked to the document's main content.

<footer>

The HTML <footer> function is used to build a footer for the sectioning root or sectioning material closest to it. A <footer> usually includes details regarding the section's creator, copyright information, or links to relevant documents.

<header>

The HTML <header> aspect denotes introductory text, which is usually a set of introducing or navigational aids. It may have several heading features and a badge, author name, and search form, among other stuff.

<h1>, <h2>, <h3>, <h4>, <h5>, <h6. Six stages of segment headings are described by the HTML <h1> to < h6> components. The largest segment rating is <h1>, and the lowest is <h6>.

<main>

The HTML <main> feature represents the predominant content of a document's body. The core information field contains content closely linked to or draws upon a document's or application's key focus or features.

<nav>

The HTML <nav> feature denotes a part of a website that contains navigation links, either inside the document window or to other pages. Tables of contents, Menus, and indexes are all instances of navigation pages.

<section>

The HTML <section> element describes a general isolated section of a text that isn't represented by a more complex semantic element.

2.14 Text content

In between <body> opening and </body> closing tags, use HTML text modules to arrange blocks or pieces of content. These elements define the intent or layout of the material, which is essential for usability and SEO.

<blockquote>

The HTML <blockquote> Item (Block Quote Element) denotes an expanded quotation. Indentation is a popular visual representation of this (Notes for how to edit it). The cite attribute can provide a URL for the quotation's source, while the cite function can allow the source's writing.

<dd>

In a description list, the HTML <dd> variable offers a description, meaning, or significance for the preceding word (dt) (dl).

<div>

The standard container for flow material is the HTML Data Division feature (<div>). Unless it's styled with CSS, it has little influence on the material or structure (e.g., styling can be applied to it).

<dl>

A summary list is represented by the HTML <dl> variable. The element contains a set of term classes (specified with the <dt> element) as well as definitions (provided by <dt> elements). This feature is often used to introduce a dictionary or view metadata (a list of pair key-value).

<dt>

The HTML <dt> object is used to specify a concept in a summary or specification list and that it must be used within an <dl> element.

<figcaption>

A tag or legend detailing the remainder of its parent figure item attributes is represented either by HTML <figcaption> or the "Figure Caption" element.

<figure>

The <figure> tag in HTML is used to represent a statistic. The (Figure with Alternate Caption) element denotes self-contained material that may have an optional caption defined by the <figcaption> element.

<hr>

A thematic split between paragraph-level items is represented by the HTML <hr> element: a changing scene in a tale or a shift of subject within a segment.

< li>

The li> element in HTML is used to display a list object.

<ol>

An organized list of items is represented by the HTML <ol> variable, usually represented as a numbered list.

<p>

A paragraph is represented by the HTML <p> variable.

<pre>

The HTML <pre> node denotes preformatted text that should be shown as it appears in the HTML code.

<ul>

The unordered list of objects, usually made as a bulleted list, is represented by the HTML <ul> variable.

2.15 Inline text semantics

The HTML inline content semantic was used to describe the context, form, or style of an expression, line, or another random piece of text.

<a>

The href attribute on the HTML <a> tag (or anchor element) provides a hyperlink to internet sites, directories, email addresses, page locations, or something else a URL may answer.

<abbr>

An acronym or abbreviation is represented by the HTML Abbreviation feature (<abbr>). The additional title attribute may include an expansion or definition for the abbreviation.

<b>

The HTML Bring More attention to component (<b>) is used to attract the viewer's interest to material that isn't given special emphasis elsewhere.

<bdi>

The HTML two-directional Isolate feature (<bdi>) instructs the bidirectional algorithm in the browser to handle the text it includes separately from the surrounding text.

<bdo>

The HTML two-directional script Override feature (bdo>) overrides the text's current directionality and renders the text in a separate direction.

**
**

The <br> feature in HTML creates a line break in document (carriage-return). It's helpful when writing poetry or an address where the line division is essential.

<cite>

The HTML Citation feature (<cite>) is used to denote a connection to a cited artistic work, and the title of the work must be included.

<code>

The HTML <code> feature styles its contents to show that the document is a short piece of computer code.

<data>

The <data> feature in HTML connects a piece of text to a machine-readable translation. The time factor must be used whether the material is time or date-related.

<dfn>

The HTML Description variable (<dfn>) denotes the word being described as a defining word or sentence.

<em>

The HTML <em> aspect denotes text with a strong focus on it. The <em> aspect may be nesting, with each level representing a higher level of focus.

<i>

The HTML Idiomatic Content feature You will learn various texts separated from the regular text for various reasons, such as conversational data, technical terminology, and taxonomic designations.

<kbd>

The HTML Keyboard Input feature (<kbd>) denotes voice input, text input from the user from a keyboard, or some other data entry system with a period of inline text.

<Mark>

According to the identified passage's significance or significance in the enclosing sense, the HTML Label Text element (<mark>) reflects text labeled or highlighted for comparison or notation purposes.

<q>

The embedded text is a small inline quote, as indicated by the HTML <q> feature. The majority of current browsers do this by enclosing the document in quotation marks.

<rb>

The HTML Ruby Base (<rb>) feature separates the base text portion of a ruby annotation, which is annotated.

<rp>

The HTML Ruby Back - up Parenthesis (<rp>) element is being used to include back - up parentheses for browsers that don't accept the ruby element for displaying ruby annotations.

<rt>

The ruby text part of a ruby notation is specified by the HTML Ruby Text (<rt>) variable used to offer transcription, translation, or pronunciation details for East Asian fonts. The <rt> variable must be stored inside a ruby element at all times.

<rtc>

The HTML Ruby Script Folder (<rtc>) module includes symbolic annotations for characters in ruby of <rb> items included inside a ruby element. Both semantic (<rtc>) and pronunciation (<rt>) are possible for <rb> objects.

<ruby>

Tiny annotations made below, above, or next to base text are represented by the HTML <ruby> feature, which is typically used to display the pronunciation of Asian characters. It may also be used to annotate other document types, but this is a less popular use.

<s>

Text with such a strikethrough, and a line across it, is rendered using the HTML <s> feature. To reflect items that are no longer meaningful or correct, use the <s> variable. When signaling document edits, however, <s> is not appropriate; instead, use the ins and del components, as required.

<samp>

The HTML Sample Element (samp>) is used to encapsulate inline text that reflects a computer program's sample (or quoted) output.

<small>

Independent of its modeled presentation, the HTML <small> analysis results from side-comments and fine print, such as copyright and legal documents. By contrast, it reduces the font size of the text inside it by one size, for example, from tiny to x-small.

<snap>

The HTML <span> feature is a common inline box for phrasing material that doesn't reflect something by itself. It may be used to individuals belonging for style (using id attributes or the class) or because they have similar attribute values, such as lang.

<strong>

The HTML Strong Value Element (<strong>) denotes a high level of significance, severity, or urgency in the text. The contents are usually shown in the bold format in browsers.

< sub>

The HTML Subscript variable (<sub>) defines the inline text that should be shown as the subscript for no other purpose than typography.

<sup>

The HTML Superscript feature (<sup>) defines the inline text that should be shown as a superscript for no other purpose than typography.

<time>

The HTML <time> aspect denotes a particular time frame.

<u>

The Html Unarticulated Notation feature (<u>) represents a block of inline text that should be made with a non-textual annotation.

<var>

In a mathematical model or a programming context, the HTML Vector element (<var>) reflects the value of a variable.

<wbr>

The HTML <wbr> feature denotes a word break chance, a spot inside text where the browser will break a line even though its line-breaking laws will not otherwise break a line there.

2.16 Elements of Styling HTML

Whenever it comes to web page presentation, HTML is very minimal. It was created to be a concise way of presenting facts. Cascading Style Sheets created by W3C in December 1996 to make it easier to style HTML objects. Size and typeface for fonts, colors for text and backgrounds, arrangement of text and pictures, amount of space between border, elements and outline for elements, and various other style properties are made much easier with CSS.

2.17 Adding Styles

Style material may be added as a text file or incorporated directly into the HTML document. The three methods for adding style details to an HTML text are as follows.

- Embedded style — Uses the <style> feature in the document's head portion.
- External CSS file — This is accomplished using the <link> feature to refer to an external Style sheet.

You will go through each of these various styles of style sheets one by one in this book

External type sheets have the least concern, while style sheets get the largest. The embedded style sheet's contrasting style guidelines may take precedence over the style attribute if you define your descriptions in integrated and external CSS sheets.

2.18 Inline Styles

By placing the CSS rules immediately into the start tag, inline styles have been used to add specific guidelines to an element. The style attribute may be used to apply it to an aspect.

A set of CSS assets and meaning pairs are used in the type attribute. A semicolon (;) separates each property: value pair, much like you might appear in an integrated or exterior style sheet. However, it must all fit on one side, with no line breaks after the semicolon.

The following example shows how to change the text's color and font size:

Example

```
<h1 style="color:Blue ; font-size:29 px;">Heading </h1>

<p style="color:Yellow ; font-size:20 px;"> paragraph.</p>

<div style="color:Red ; font-size:16px;">Text </div>
```

Using inline patterns is commonly thought to be a poor idea. Since style guidelines are inserted directly within the html tag, the presentation is mingled with the document's text, making modifying and managing a website extremely challenging.

2.19 Embedded-Style Sheets

Internal style sheets, also known as embedded style sheets, only influence the paper in which they are embedded.

The <style> tag in an HTML document's head segment is used to describe embedded style sheets. Inside the <head> segment, you can specify any number of <styles> components.

The illustration below shows how style guidelines are incorporated into a web page.

Example

```
<head>
<style>
body { background-color: Yellow; }
h1 {color: Red; }
p { color: black; }
</style>
</head>
```

2.20 External-Style Sheets

If a pattern is extended to a large number of websites, an additional style sheet is ideal.

An external style sheet is a different document that contains all of the style rules, which can be linked from any Html file on your Web. External-style sheets seem to be the most versatile since they enable you to update only one file to alter the appearance of a whole website. External style sheets may be attached in two ways, connecting and importing

2.21 External-Style Sheets Are Linked

The <link> tag may be used to link an external-style sheet to an HTML text. As seen here, the <link> tag is placed within the <head> section:

Example

```
<head>
<link rel="CSS" href="html.css">
</head>
```

2.22 Importing External-Style Sheets

Another way to load an external-style sheet is to use the import rule. The import declaration tells the browser to install and use the styles from an external style sheet.

It can be seen in two forms. The easiest method is to have it in your <head> section's <style> feature. Other CSS rules can also be included in the <style> function, so keep that in mind.

Example

```
<style>
  @import URL ("html/CS.css");
  p {  color: Red;  font-size: 18px; }
</style>
```

Similarly, the @import clause may be used to insert a style sheet onto another style sheet.

Example

```
@import URL("HTML/guideline.css");
body
{
```

```
color: Red; font-size: 18px;
}
```

Chapter-3 HTML for Text Formatting

HTML contains many tags that you can use to render certain data on your websites to look different than regular text, like the following.

3.1 Bold Text (<b>)

You will see in the below example, everything that occurs inside the <b>...</b> variable is bolded.

```
 html>
<head> <title>Text Title for bold</title> </head>
<body>
<p> The is an example for <b>bold</b> text. </p>
</body>
</html>
```

It produced the result as "This is an example for **bold** text.

3.2 Italic Text (<i>)

Anything contained inside the <i>...</i> variable is italicized, as seen below.

```
<html>
<head> <title>Title for Italic</title>  </head>
<body>
<p>It is an example for <i>italicized</i> text. </p>
</body>
```

```
</html>
```

It will produce "It is an example for the *italicized* text."

3.3 Underlined Text (<u>)

All that occurs inside the <u>...</u> aspect is underlined, as seen below.

```
<html>
<head> <title>Title of Underlined </title> </head>
<body>
<p>It is an example of <u>under-lined</u> Text. </p>
</body>
</html>
```

It will produce a result "It is an example of **under-line** text."

3.4 Strike Text (<strike>)

Strikethrough is used to view something that occurs inside the <strike>...</strike> element, which is a fine line across the text as seen below.

```
<html>
<head>
<title>Title strike Text </title>
</head>
<body> <p>It is an example of <strike>strike</strike> text. </p>
```

```
</body>
```

```
</html>
```

It will produce a result "It is an example of ~~strike~~ text."

3.5 Monospaced Font (<tt>)

A <tt>...</tt> element's content is composed in monospaced font. Since various letters have different height (for example, the letter's' is larger than the letter, fonts are classified as variable-width fonts). Each letter in a monospaced text, on the other hand, is the same distance.

```
<html>
```

```
<head>  <title> Title for Monospaced </title>  </head>
```

```
<body>
```

```
<p>It is an example of <tt>monospaced</tt> text. </p>
```

```
</body>
```

```
</html>
```

It will produce the result "It is an example of monospaced text."

3.6 Superscript Text (<sup>)

The text of a ^{...} variable is composed in superscript; the fonts is the same as the surrounding characters, except it is shown halves a character's height over them.

```
<html>
```

```
<head><title>Title for Super_script</title></head>
```

```
<body><p>It is an example of <sup>super_script</sup>text.</p>
```

```
</body>
```

```
</html>
```

It will produce a result. "It is an example of ^{superscript} text

3.7 Subscript Text (<sub>)

A _{...} element's text is typed in subscript; the text size is the same as the surrounding characters, but it is shown halves a character's height under the other characters.

```
<html>
```

```
<head> <title>Title Subscript </title> </head>
```

```
<body>
```

```
<p>It is an example of <sub>subscript</sub> text. </p>
```

```
</body>
```

```
</html>
```

It will produce a result "It is an example of subscript text."

3.8 Inserted Text (<ins>)

Inserted text is something that occurs inside the ins>.../ins> element.

```
<html>
```

```
<head> <title> Title for Inserted Text</title> </head>
```

```
<body>
```

```
<p>It is an example of <del>delete</del> <ins>inserted </ins> text </p>
```

```
</body>
```

```
</html>
```

It will produce a result "It is an example of inserted text."

3.9 Deleted Text (<del>)

All text inside the <del>...</del> function is shown as removed text.

```
<html>
```

```
<head> <title>Deleted </title> </head>
```

```
<body>
```

```
<p>It is an example of <del>delete</del> <ins>and inserted </ins> text
```
```
</p>
```

```
</body>
```

```
</html>
```

It will produce a result "It is an example of inserted text."

3.10 Larger Text (<big>)

The text of the <big>...</big> feature is one font size greater than that of the remaining of the text containing it.

```
<html>
```

```
<head> <title>Title for larger text</title> </head>
```

```
 <body>
```

```
<p>It is an example of <big>larger</big>text. </p>
```

```
</body>
```

```
</html>
```

It will produce a result "It is an example of larger text."

3.11 Smaller Text (<small>)

The text of the <small>...</small> feature is one font smaller size than that of the remaining text surrounding it.

```
<html>
```

```
<head> <title> Title for small text </title> </head>
```

```
<body>
```

```
p>It is an example of <small>small</small >text. </p></body>
```

```
</html>
```

It will produce a result "It is an example of small text."

3.12 Grouping Content (<div> <span>)

You may use the <div> and <span> elements to link elements together to construct parts or sections of a list.

E.g. all of the endnotes on a website may be included inside a <div> element to show that all of the items inside that <div> element are related to the footnotes. You may then apply a style to the <div> feature to make them look according to a collection of guidelines.

```
<html>
```

```
<head> <title>The Example</title> </head>
```

```
<body>

<div id = "List" align = "middle" >

<a href = "/index.htm">Page</a> |

<a href = "/about/contact_us.htm">Phone</a> |

<a href = "/about/index.htm">Why US</a>

</div>

<div id = "content" align = "left" >

<h5>HTML programming</h5>

<p>Just a practice.....</p>

</div>

</body>

</html>
```

It will produce the result

Page | Phone | Why US

HTML programming

Just a practice.....

In contrast, the <span> element is only used to combine inline objects. If you have a section of a paragraph that you want to combine together, you may do so with the <span> function, as seen below.

```
<html>

<head> <title>Span </title> </head>
```

```
<body>
```

```
<p>It is the example of <span style = "color: Purple">span_tag</span>
```

```
and the <span style = "color: red">div tag</span> along with .CSS</p>
```

```
</body>
```

```
</html>
```

It will produce the following result

It is the example of the span tag and the div tag along with CSS

3.12 Emphasized Text (<em>)

Everything that appears within the <em>...</em> element is highlighted text.

```
<html>
```

```
<head> <title> Title for Emphasized Text</title> </head>
```

```
<body>
```

```
<p>It is an example of  <em>emphasized</em> text.</p>
```

```
</body>
```

```
</html>
```

It shows the result "It is an example of *emphasized* text."

3.13 Marked Text (<mark>)

Anything inside the <mark>...</mark> feature is labelled with Red ink and shown as such.

```
<html>
```

```
<head> <title>Title of Marked Text</title> </head>
```

```
<body> <p>It is an example of <mark>marked</mark> with Red </p>
```

```
</body>
```

```
</html>
```

It will produce the result "It is an example of marked with a red."

3.14 Strong Text (<strong>)

All inside the <strong>...</strong> aspect is treated as essential text.

```
<html>
```

```
<head> <title> Title of Strong </title> </head>
```

```
<body>
```

```
<p>It is an example of <strong>strong</strong> text. </p>
```

```
</body>
```

```
</html>
```

It will produce a result

It is an example of **strong** text.

3.15 Abbreviation (<abbr>)

Placed a text within the opening <abbr> and closing </abbr> tags to abbreviate it. If current, the title element must only include this complete summary.

```
<html>
<head> <title>Abbreviation's title</title> </head>
<body>
<p>It is an example of abbreviation <abbr title = "United states of America">USA</abbr>. </p>
</body>
</html>
```

It will produce a result "It is an example of abbreviation USA."

3.16 Text Direction (<bdo>)

Bi-Directional Override <bdo>...</bdo> is an element that is used to bypass that current text direction.

```
<html>
<head> <title>Title of Direction</title> </head>
<body>
<p>Test Text L-R. </p>
<p><bdo dir = "rtl">Text R-L . </bdo></p>
</body>
</html>
```

It will produce the result

Test from left to right.

.tfel ot thgir txeT

3.17 Special Terms (<dfn>)

You should use the <dfn>...</dfn> component (or HTML Description Element) to indicate that you're adding a new word. It's equivalent to using italics in the middle of a document. The <dfn> function is typically used to introduce a main word for the first time. The text of a <dfn> element is usually rendered in italic font in modern browsers.

```
<html>
<head><title>Title Special</title></head>
<body>
<p>It is an example
</body>
</html>
```

It will produce "It is an example of *special* Text."

3.18 Quoting Text (<blockquote>)

If you wish to quote something from another source, place it between the <blockquote>...</blockquote> tags. Text within a blockquote> feature is normally indented from the surrounding text's left and right sides, and italicized font is often used.

```
<html>
<head>
<title>Title Blockquote</title>
</head>
```

```
<body>

<p> First, it is a good idea to maintain order and structure in your HTML
documents. </ p>

<blockquote> Avoid overloading your pages with heavy images and other
fancy stuff you have found on the Internet. </blockquote>

</body>

</html>
```

It will produce a result

First, it is a good idea to maintain order and structure in your HTML documents.

Avoid overloading your pages with heavy images and other fancy stuff you have found on the Internet.

3.19 Short Quotations (<q>)

When you want to insert a double quotation within a sentence, use the
<q>...</q> feature.

```
<html>

<head><title>Title</title></head>

<body>

<p>It is an example, <q>Double Quotations</q>.</p>

</body>

</html>
```

It will produce a result

It is an example, "Double Quotations."

3.20 Text Citations (<cite>)

If you're citing something, you should put the source between the opening <cite> and closing </cite> tags.

The output of the <cite> feature is made in italicized text by contrast, as it would be in a print publication.

```
<html>
<head> <title>Title</title> </head>
<body>
<p>It is an example <cite>Text citations</cite>. </p>
</body>
</html>
```

It will produce the result. "It is an example *Text citation.*"

3.21 Computer Code (<code>)

All programming code that will occur on a Website page should be enclosed by a <code>...</code> extension. The <code> element's material is usually displayed in a monospaced text.

```
<html>
<head> <title>Title of Code </title> </head>
<body>
<p>Text. <code>It is an example code. </code> Text. </p>
</body>
```

```
</html>
```

It will produce the result. "Text. It is an example code. Text."

3.22 Keyboard Text (<kbd>)

If you're talking about computers, you can use the <kbd>...</kbd> element to mean what must be typed in, as in this case.

```
<html>
<head> <title>Title Keyboard</title></head>
<body>
<p>Text. <kbd>It is an example </kbd> Text. </p>
</body>
</html>
```

It will produce a result Text. It is an example Text."

3.23 Programming Variables (<pre> <code>)

This element is usually used in conjunction with the <pre> and <code> components to indicate that the form of the function is a vector.

```
<html>
<head> <title>Title For Example</title> </head>
<body>
<p><code>File. Code ("<var>User. Name </var>")</code></p>
</body>
```

```
</html>
```

It will produce the result "File. Code ("*User. Name* ")"

3.24 Program Output (<samp>)

The <samp>...</samp> variable specifies a sample result from a software, document, or other source. It's mostly used to log programming and coding principles.

```
<html>
<head> <title>Title Example</title> </head>
<body>
<p>It is an example a program <samp>Output </samp></p>
</body>
</html>
```

It will produce the result "It is an example of a program output Output!"

3.25 Address Text (<address>)

Any address is contained in the <address>...</address> element.

```
<html>
<head> <title>Address Title </title> </head>
<body>
<address>B-IV 451 street 4 New York USA </address>
</body>
```

```
</html>
```

It will produce "*B-IV 451 street 4 New York USA*"

3.26 Acronym (<acronym>)

You will use the <acronym> element tag to show that the text within the <acronym> and </acronym> Tags is an acronym. Typically, several browsers do not alter the appearance of the <acronym> element's material.

```
<html>
<head> <title>Title of Acronym </title> </head>
<body>
<p>It is an example of <acronym> acronym </acronym></p>
</body>
</html>
```

It will show the result "It is an example of the acronym."

3.27 Comments

A comment would be a block of code that no web viewer displays. It is common sense to include comments in the HTML document file, particularly when working with complicated HTML documents. Comments are used to denote the different parts of an Html file and some other details regarding the code that might be useful to someone working at the code. Comments also aid in the understanding of the code by yourself and others and increase the readability of your code.

Between the !—... --> tags, HTML comments are held. As a result, any code or note inserted inside the !—... --> tags will be immediately interpreted as a comment, and the browser will disregard it and not show it.

```
<html>
<head> <! --Started header here-->
<title> Title here </title>
</head> <! – Header End -->
<body>
<p>Html coding here.... </p>
</body>
</html>
```

It will show the result "Html coding here..."

If you have noticed in the code, you placed the certain text in between the comment tag and when you check the output, it doesn't get displayed in the document. The browser did not display it because it read it as a comment so it ignored it when it was displaying the rest of the content.

3.28 HTML Comment Types and Formats

HTML comments come in a variety of forms and formats, including:

- Conditional Comments
- Comment Suffix
- Multiline Comments
- Commenting Style
- Commenting Script

Chapter-4: HTML Images, Tables, list and blocks

Images, list blocks, and tables are essential for creating Html files and straightforwardly describing several abstract topics on your website. In this part, you'll go into how to use photos on web pages in easy steps.

4.1 Insert Image

Using the <img> suffix, you may add any picture to your web page. The basic syntax for using this HTML tag is as follows.

`<img src = "URL of image" ... attributes/>`

The <img> is a void tag, that ensures it can only include a certain set of attributes and has no closing tag.

```
<html>
<head><title> Image in Page</title>
</head>
<body><p>Image-Insert</p>
<img src = "Google/axy.png" alt = "Image" />
</body>
</html>
```

You may use a JPEG, GIF or PNG image file depending on your preference; make sure the src attribute contains the right image file name. The picture name is case sensitive at all times. The <alt> HTML attribute is a required element attribute that specifies an alternative text for the picture if it cannot be viewed due to a network issue.

4.2 Set Image Location

You usually hold all of the photographs in a separate directory. So, let's put your Html document image.html in your home directory and make a subdirectory image within the home directory for our test.png document.

```
<html>
<head> <title>Image in page</title>
</head>
<body> <p>Simple Image Insert</p>
<img src = "thegoogleicon.png" alt = "Image" />
</body>
</html>
```

4.3 Set the image's width and height.

The height and width attributes enable you to dynamically define the height and width of a picture depending on how you would like it to look. You may also specify the image's width and height in pixels or as a percentage of the actual dimension.

```
<html>
<head>
<title> width and height. </title></head>
<body> <p> width and height. </p>
<img src = "thegoogleicon.png" alt = "Image" width = "250" height = "120"/>
</body>
```

4.4 Image Border

The picture would have some kind of borders around it by default; however, you may directly set the border depth of the image using the borders attribute of the <img> class. Giving an image a thickness of zero, for example, implies there would be no boundary around the image.

```html
<html>
 <head>
   <title>Image Border</title></head>
<body><p> image Border</p>
<img src = "thegoogleicon.png" alt = "Image" border = "5"/>
</body>
</html>
```

4.5 HTML Tables

Tables in HTML enable web developers to view data in columns and rows of table cells, such as text, photos, connections, and other tables. The <table> HMTL tag is used to construct HTML tables, with the <tr> tag used to create table rows and the <td> tag used to create table data cells. All of the elements under <td> are standard and, by contrast, left-aligned.

```html
<html> <head>
<title>Title_Tables</title></head>
```

```
<body><table_border = "2">
```

```
<tr><td>R-A, C-A</td><td>R-B, C-B</td>
```

```
</tr><tr><td>R-B C-A</td><td>R-B, C-B</td></tr>
```

```
</table>
```

```
</body>
```

```
</html>
```

It will show the result

R-1, C-1	R-2, C-2
R-2, C-1	R-2, C-2

The border text within the table tag is an element of the <table> tag in this case, and it's used to apply a border to all of the table cells as defined in the border attribute. If a border isn't what you're looking for, just use border = "0."

4.6 Table Heading

The <th> tag may be used to describe the table heading. As a result, this tag would be used to substitute the <td> tag, which is primarily used to reflect the table data cell. You can always make your tabletop row the table heading, as seen in the illustration below. Otherwise, you may use the <th> variable in either row. The default behavior of headings specified in the <th> tag is for them to be oriented and bold.

```
<html>
```

```
<head>
```

```
<title>Table Heading </title> </head>
```

```
<body>
```

```
<table border = "2">
```

```
<tr><th>St-Name</th><th>marks</th></tr>
```

```
<tr><td>Ali Raman</td><td>500</td></tr>
```

```
<tr><td>Ali Hussain</td><td>890</td></tr></table>
```

```
</body>
```

```
</html>
```

It will show the result

St-Name	marks
Ali Raman	500
Ali Hussain	890

4.7 Cellpadding and Cells pacing Attributes

To set the blank space in the table cells, you'll use two attributes named cell-spacing and cell-padding. The cell spacing property specifies the distance between cell-padding and table cells, specifies the distance between a cell's boundaries and its text.

```
<html>
```

```
<head><title>Cellpadding</title>
```

```
</head>
```

```
<body>
```

```
<table border = "2" cellpadding = "12" cellspacing = "12">
```

```
<tr><th>St.Name</th><th>Marks</th></tr>

<tr> <td>Ali Raman</td><td>580</td></tr>

<tr><td>Ali Hussain</td><td>980</td></tr>

</table> </body> </html>
```

It will show the following result.

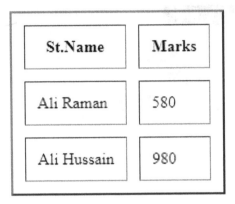

4.8 HTML List

Web developers have three options for viewing data-filled lists in HTML. One or even more list elements are required in all HTML lists. Lists may include the following items:

- <ul> (unordered list): Using simple bullets to represent objects in lists.

- <ol>: A numbered list. To show your list info, this uses a variety of numbers.

- <dl>: A compilation of definitions. It organizes the list of objects in the same way a dictionary does.

4.9 HTML Unordered Lists

The unordered lists are a set of similar objects that are not arranged or sequenced in any particular way. The HTML <ul> tag may be used to construct this kind of list. A bullet is shown next to each object in the unordered chart.

```
<html>
<head>
<title>Unordered</title>
</head><body>
<ul><li>        Chapter-1</li>        <li>Chapter-2</li><li>Chapter-3</li>
<li>Chapter-4</li>   </ul>
</body>
</html>
```

It will show the result as

- Chapter-1
- Chapter-2
- Chapter-3
- Chapter-4

4.10 The type listing attribute

It is a HTML attribute for the <ul> tag that specifies the bullet type you want the list items to have. A disc is the default list form. The following are also the bullet styles that are available:

```
<ul type = "Circle"><ul type = "disc"> <ul type = "Square">
<html>
<head><title>Title of Unordered</title></head>
```

```html
<body>
<ul type = "square">
<li>Chapter-1</li> <li>Chapter-2</li>
<li>Chapter-3</li> <li>Chapter-4</li>
</ul>
<ul type = "disc">
<li>Chapter-5</li><li>Chapter-6</li>
<li>Chapter-7</li><li>Chapter-8</li>
</ul>
<ul type = "circle">
<li>Chapter-9</li><li>Chapter-10</li>
<li>Chapter-11</li><li>Chapter-12</li>
</ul>
</body></html>
```

- Chapter-1
- Chapter-2
- Chapter-3
- Chapter-4

- Chapter-5
- Chapter-6
- Chapter-7
- Chapter-8

- Chapter-9
- Chapter-10
- Chapter-11
- Chapter-12

4.11 HTML Ordered Lists

If you like to see the lists in an amount or sorted layout instead of unordered or bulleted, use the HTML organized list file. This set was made with the <ol> HTML tag. The numbering of the list begins at one and continues to grow for each subsequent organized list component with the <li> tag.

```html
<html> <head>
<title> Ordered List</title>
</head>
<body><ol>
<li>Chapter-1</li><li>Chapter-2</li>
<li>Chapter-3</li><li>Chapter-1</li>
</ol></body>
</html>
```

1. Chapter-1
2. Chapter-2
3. Chapter-3
4. Chapter-1

Chapter-5: Links, Fonts, Multimedia, Frames & Iframes

In this chapter, you will learn Links, Fonts, Multimedia, Frames & Iframes in HTML.

5.1 Text Links

A website also includes several links that lead to other sites or even separate parts of the same page. Hyperlinks are the different types of links.

Hyperlinks enable users to navigate different websites on the Internet by simply clicking on terms, sentences, or images. As a result, you'll learn how to build hyperlinks from text or photographs on a webpage.

5.2 Linking Documents

An HTML tag is used to specify a connection. This tag is known as the anchor tag, and everything between the starting tag and the terminating tag becomes a component of the connection, which a user may press to access the connected text. The basic notation for using tag is as follows.

```
<html>
<head> <title> Linking Documents </title> </head>
<body> <p>Just Click</p>
<a href = "https://www.facebook.com" target = "FB">Facebook</a>
</body>
</html>
```

5.3 Target Attributes

In our previous case, you made use of the goal attribute. This attribute defines the condition in which the associated document is opened. The below are the possibilities:

- blank: The associated Text would be opened in a new tab
- self: It opens the related text in the same window as the current one.
- Parent: It will open the file in the parent window that is connected.
- top: This will show the associated text in the window's whole body.
- Open the linked file in a specified target window with this option.

```
<html>
<head>
<title>Title for example </title>
<base href = "https://www.google.com/"></head>
 <body>        <p>Just Click </p>
<a href = "/html/Facebook.htm" target = "_blank">Opens in New</a>
</body>
</html>
```

5.4 Base Path

It is unnecessary to include a whole URL for each connection when linking HTML documents to an analogous website. If you use the <base> tag in the File header, you'll be able to avoid it. This tag is used to include a common route for all connections. As a result, your browser can combine the assigned relative path with the current base path to form an entire URL.

```
<html>
```

```
<head>
```

```
<title>Title for example </title>
```

```
<base href = "https://www.google.com/"></head>
```

```
<body><p>Just Click </p>
```

```
<a href = "/html/Facebook.htm" target = "_blank">Opens in New</a>
```

```
</body>
```

```
</html>
```

Linking to a Section of a Page. The name attribute may be used to build a path to a certain portion of a webpage. It's a two-step procedure.

To begin, build a connection to the location you want to visit inside a website and label it by using the tag as follows:

```
<h1>Linking <a name = "Bottom"></a></h1>
```

The second move is to create a hyperlink between the text and the location where you want to go:

```
<a href = "www.google.com">Go to the Bottom</a>
```

5.5 Link Colors setting

Using the connect, vlink and alink, attributes of the <body> tag, you can actually determine the colors of your active and visited links.

```
<html>
```

```
<head> <title>Linking Title </title>
```

```
<base href = "https://google.com/">
```

```
</head>
```

```
<body alink = "#256850" link = "#141414" vlink = "#F41533">
<p>Click</p>
<a href = "www.google.com" target = "_blank" >HTML link</a>
</body>
</html>
```

5.6 HTML Fonts

Fonts are critical to rendering a web more user-friendly and improving page readability. The font face and color are largely dependent on the device and browser being used to display your article; however, you can style, scale, and color the text on your site using the HTML <font> suffix. A <basefont> tag may make all text the same height, face, and color.

To configure the fonts, use the Font Tag's height, color, and face attributes. Simply use the font> tag to modify all of the typeface attributes on your website at any time. The text after that would not alter until you close the tag with the </font> tag. Inside a single <font> tag, you can modify one or more of the font attributes.

5.7 Set Font Size

The size attribute may be used to change the font size of the text. The agreed values vary from 1 (smallest) to 7 (largest) (largest). A font's default size is three.

```
<html>
<head> <title>Font_Size</title></head>
```

```html
<body><font size="7">size ="7"</font><br />
<font size = "6">size = "6"</font><br />
<font size = "5">Size = "5"</font><br />
<font size = "4">size= "4"</font><br />
<font size = "3">size ="3"</font><br />
<font size = "2">size = "2"</font><br />
<font size = "1">size = "1"</font>
</body>
</html>
```

size = "7"

size = "6"

Size = "5"

size = "4"

size = "3"

size = "2"

size = "1"

5.8 Relative Font Size

You may choose how many sizes bigger or smaller the font should be than the norm. You may use font size = <"-n"> or font size =< "+n"> to define the font size.

```
<html>
```

```
<head><title>Font_Style</title></head>
```

```
<body><font size="+4">size ="+4"</font><br />
<font size="+3">size="+3"</font><br />
<font size="+2">size="+2"</font><br />
<font size = "+1">size = "+1"</font><br />
<font size ="-1">size ="-1"</font>
</body></html>
```

size = "+4"

size = "+3"

size = "+2"

size = "+1"

size = "-1"

5.9 Font Face Setting

You may use the face attribute to change the glyph face, but keep in mind that if the consumer will not have the font enabled, they didn't manage to see it. Instead, the consumer would be presented with the computer's default font face.

```
<html>
<head><title>Face_font </title></head>
<body>
<font face ="Times New Roman" size = "5">Times New Roman</font><br
/>
<font face="Bed_rock"size="5">Bed_rock</font><br />
</body></html>
```

Times New Roman
Bedrock

5.10 Font Color Setting

The colour attribute within the font> tag may be used to change the colour of your font while it is shown. You may also define the colour you like by typing in the name of a colour or its hex code.

```
<html>
<head>
<title>Font Color</title></head><body>
<font color = "#FF0000">This text is in pink</font><br />
```

```
<font color = "Blue">This text is Blue</font>

</body>

</html>
```

This text is in pink
This text is Blue

5.11 HTML – Frames

HTML frames are often used to divide the browser window into several parts, each of which can view and load a different HTML document. A frameset is a collection of frames inside a browser window. The window is divided into frames in the same manner as the tables are divided into rows and columns.

5.12 Disadvantages of Frames

There are a few drawbacks of using frames in your web pages so that you can avoid them at all costs:

- Certain smaller computers are unable to handle frames because their screens are insufficiently wide to separate.
- Because of differences in screen resolutions, your page can appear differently on different computers.
- The back button on the browser would not function as anticipated.
- Frame technology is still not supported by a lot of browsers.

5.13 Creating Frames

You use the <frameset> tag instead of the <body> tag use the frames. The <frameset> tag specifies how the window can be divided into frames. Horizontal frames are defined by the row's attributes of the <frameset> suffix, whereas the cols attribute defines vertical frames. Each frame is identified by the <frame> tag, which specifies which HTML document will be shown in the frame.

As an example

An explanation of how to make three horizontal frames is as follows:

```
<html>
<head><title> Frames</title> </head>
<frameset rows = "20%,85%,20%"> <frame_name = "right" src = "www.google.com" /> <frame name = "About" src = "google.com" /> <frame_name = "top" src = "www.google.com" /> <noframes>
<body>Frame is here </body> </no_frames> </frame_set> </html>
```

5.14 iframe

By using the HTML tag <iframe>, you can build an inline frame. The <iframe> tag isn't linked to the <frameset> tag in any way; instead, it may appear everywhere in your code. The <iframe> tag is in charge of identifying an oblong segment inside the document where the browser will view a different document, complete with scrollbars and borders. An iframe is used To insert one document in the other document.

5.16 Src

This attribute specifies the name of the file to be enabled in the frame. Any URL may be used as its value. Src = "www.google/top.htm" will, for example, open an HTML file from the HTML directory.

5.17 name

You may assign a frame a name with this attribute. It is used to specify the frame in which a text should be loaded. It is particularly useful when creating links in one frame that load websites in another frame since the second frame requires a name to mark itself as the link's destination.

5.18 frame border

This attribute determines whether or not the frame's boundaries are visible; whether one is specified, it takes precedence over the value specified and in-frame order attribute also on <frameset> name, which may take one of two values: 1 (yes) or 0 (no) (no).

5.19 margin width

This attribute helps define the area's base between the frame's boundaries and the substance on the left side. Pixels are used to express the value. For instance, margin width = "20."

5.20 margin height

This feature helps define the area's size between the frame's boundaries and its contents at the top and bottom. Pixels are used to express the value. For instance, margin height = "15" is a good example.

5.21 height

This attribute defines the height of an iframe.

5.22 scrolling

This attribute regulates the presence of the scrollbars on the frame. The accepts one of three values: "yes," "no," or "auto." Scrolling = "no" suggests that there should be no scroll bars.

5.23 <longdesc

You may use this attribute to include a path to another page that contains a detailed summary of the frame's contents. <longdesc = "frame.html" is an example.

5.24 width

This attribute defines the width of an iframe.

5.25 Advanced Features:

HTML is a pretty simple code to use, so much so that if people have a clear understanding, they leap right into creating web pages without considering much about HTML's basics.

As a result, most web developers are squandering their time and resources by not fully using HTML and CSS, rendering their lives more complicated.

The distinction between abstract and actual tags is among the most important basic principles in HTML that once grasped, can have a significant effect on a web designer's workflow.

Conclusion

My friends, this little book has already come to a close. While I hope that you will be able to use HTML "off the shelf" in your area, you will be satisfied if it merely sparks your curiosity. The approaches outlined in this book are among the most important ways for HTML users at all levels to improve their efficiency and proficiency. Consider if you and your teammates can and should utilize these – and other opportunities that will inevitably become available – to maximize performance. This book is intended for those who are new to the field. You also attempted to address the following topics in this book, which are equally essential for beginners and professionals:

- HTML for Beginners – all you need to talk about HTML in one location

- An overview of how HTML utilizes tags to identify the content of web pages

- Ideas on how to best design the template of your web pages

- Strategies for modifying the styles, fonts, and colors of elements

- A look into how you can connect with the web page users using forms and input boxes

- Examples of how to put what you've learned into practice when you create websites

- Formatting, scaling, fonts, graphics, gradients, multimedia, shapes, sprites, and – all the resources you need to customize your website fully!